INTERVIEW FOR LIFE

ENCOURAGE • MOTIVATE • CHALLENGE

NIKKI FONTENOT
creator of the *Interview For Life* program

authorHOUSE®

AuthorHouse™
1663 Liberty Drive
Bloomington, IN 47403
www.authorhouse.com
Phone: 1-800-839-8640

Published by AuthorHouse   07/31/2012

ISBN: 978-1-4685-9614-4 (sc)
ISBN: 978-1-4685-9615-1 (e)

Library of Congress Control Number: 2012907785

Any people depicted in stock imagery provided by Thinkstock are models, and such images are being used for illustrative purposes only.
Certain stock imagery © Thinkstock.

This book is printed on acid-free paper.

CONTENTS

WHY WRITE THIS BOOK?

This book is based on the actual *Interview For Life* program, which is a combination of career skills and life skills presented in a workshop setting. The book provides enough information to get you thinking and started on a path that will help you increase your chances of being successful and professional. It does not, however, overwhelm you with so much information that would cause you to put down the book after struggling through the first chapter. There is plenty of information available out there on these topics; this book is designed to be a pocket guide packed with succinct, practical guidance.

I encourage and challenge you to dream and live your best life! But first, you have to figure out what that is!

Over the years I had been asked, "Why don't you write a book about the *Interview For Life* program?" My thought was, "Great idea!" Then I could reach more people and show how creating this program and implementing it into our local school system was one way to mix ideas with talents and make a difference. I saw a need and I got creative. So many people want to see change; to make change happen, you have to start somewhere and do something.

In my experience of meeting people while teaching this program, I realize people of all ages need this information.

I would also get asked by classes that received *Interview for Life* training, "Later on in the year, can you come back to our class and do a reminder session?" Well, with this book, you can carry these reminders around with you.

Just for fun, throughout this book, I revisit a few "off the wall" situations when I witnessed total unprofessionalism. Being unprofessional is just one of the areas we will cover in the next few pages. Next time you are in a store, listen to what the checkout clerks are talking about out loud and in front of you. How are you greeted while shopping? Have you ever had to wait until a store employee gets off of her cell phone to have your question answered? If we don't expect professionalism, then we will never get it!

If you are not preparing yourself and creating a plan to accomplish your goals, then you may never get off of life's first base. If you are not prepared for the interview process and do not know what to expect from the interviewer, or how to market yourself, you could lose the chance of employment.

Today is your day! Make it happen! Increase the quality of your life!

Nikki Fontenot

This book is dedicated to all of the students, past and present, who have used the *Interview For Life* program to push themselves to be their best!

Thank you . . .

To all of our sponsors who partner with *IFL* each year to bring this program to our schools.

To all of the teachers and administrators who have trusted their classes to us year after year.

To my husband Ryan, who supports each and every idea I have and encourages me to go for it!

To my daughters, Maci and Ellie Kate, for giving me a reason to work harder to realize our family dreams.
To my parents for giving me encouragement as I worked through this creative process and forever saying
"you can do it!"

A special thank you to my team who helped edit and proof this project: Dana Bridges, Shayne Laughlin, Felicia Hall, and Peter O'Carroll.

CHAPTER ONE

Your Blueprint

Okay, let's get started! You will need a piece of paper and something to write with.

Do you know what a blueprint is? Webster's defines it as "a detailed plan or program of action." So what is your blueprint? Who are you? What are your interests? What makes you tick? What makes you get out of bed in the morning?

Our world is so busy. We get caught up running errands, taking care of our families, working at our jobs, going to school, and sometimes running in circles looking for the right path. We don't ever really stop to think about what we really want in our lives. More than anything else, you need to find a path that leads you to a great life and successful career.

What are you interested in? Do you have a hobby? What values and beliefs are important to you? All of these questions have important answers! They shape and define who we are. How can you go forth and be happy if you don't know what it will take to make you happy? Know your blueprint so that you can create your effective plan.

Here are more questions to consider when drawing your blueprint.

- Are you an inside person or do you love the outdoors?
- Do you love working with animals?
- Are you interested in the medical profession?
- Are you good at solving problems?
- Are you good with numbers?
- Are you a people person or would you rather work behind the scenes?
- Are you creative with your hands?
- Do you like to travel or would you rather stay home most of the time?
- What are your talents?
- What things come easily to you?
- What do you have that can be shared with others?

In life it's helpful to know what you want, set goals, and then put together steps to get there. In my experience, it has been helpful to write the steps down so I stay reminded of my goals. Then even when I don't see the results right away, I see the list of steps getting smaller.

Motivate yourself in small steps. This will build true, solid self-confidence. You will see accomplishments, and that's good for any mind. I have learned that the more I work on me as a whole person, then better mom, wife, daughter, friend, and business woman I become.

Defining who we are—and what makes us happy—is important in life and on the job. Research shows that a happier person in general is a more productive employee.

Most of us need to work to provide quality of life for our families or simply to pay the bills.

I don't mind working; however, it's important to me to make a difference at the same time. It only took me until I was in my 30s to figure this out! I have always been self-motivated and driven, and these are great qualities to have. However, early on I didn't know the direction I wanted to go in my life, so I didn't know where to apply my best qualities. When I was younger I thought I would grow up and be a recording artist. Then, as I played tennis for my college, I thought I would be a big tennis star. Interestingly enough, I don't remember a time between high school and college where I ever stopped to think about what I really wanted to do with my life. I never stopped to think about how important my talents and interests really were. Picking a major doesn't always mean it's something we are truly interested in and really want to do for the rest of our lives. Most of us pick a job or career that pays well, has benefits, and is hiring! Later on we will discuss *jobs* vs. *careers*, but for now just keep in mind they are different and serve different purposes.

Are you ready to think? Ready to dream? The goals and dreams you have don't care where you come from. They care whether you have what it takes to reach and accomplish them! Right now you need to realize you are powerful and talented. You can make your life great; it just takes work. Here we go.

On your paper list three job or career options you would like to have (or areas you would like to study) and why you chose those areas. *Why* you chose the job, career path, or area of study is the most important part. List what you would like to do and why. For those of you who have already figured out *the one* area you want to study or work in, list the reasons why you chose *that* area.

1. _____
2. _____
3. _____

Now, look at your choices. Do you have a true interest in these areas? Did you pick a specific area of work because your father and grandfather did this? That is fine if it is what you really want to do for the next several decades. Are any of these options something that will allow you to use one of your talents? We all have talents and things that come naturally to us. You have to tap into them. Is there a skill that can be applied to one of these options to set you on a career or job path? If you have an interest in what you do, you will enjoy what you do, increase your chances of doing a better job and very possibly increase the quality of your life. If you have a true love and interest for music, but not so much on the talent side, do you still pursue this as a career? Probably not, but you could always include it in your life as a hobby. Look for something else that you know you could get a job doing that you have a true interest in—and have more enjoyable days at work!

One day when you have a hard day at work, I want you to think back, dig deep, and remember why you chose this job, career choice, or area of study. It will be a huge benefit if you are passionate about what you do. If you are not, then try to find something that you can do through your job to make a difference in the community or in someone's life.

CHAPTER TWO

Exercise Your Mind

This is one of my favorite parts of the *Interview For Life* program. It's where your vision starts!

You must have a vision and know that you are destined to do great things!

Have you ever thought that there might be a bigger plan for your life than the one you are living right now? I believe we all have a mission if we are willing to answer the call. Part of our journey is to take one road at a time, believing that it will then lead to the next road that is part of the great plan. You must believe in yourself if you want others to believe in you. To dream is to keep your creative mind alive!

Here is where I want you to think about the questions I asked you in Chapter One. Close your eyes and dream of the life you want to build. I use the word "build" because your dream doesn't usually happen by poofy dust. (I wish it were that easy!) Take a few minutes and stop reading. Just close your eyes and begin your vision. Take five minutes if you need to. Here are a few examples of things to get your imagination moving.

- Do you have a good job?
- Are you building your financial future?
- Are you being challenged intellectually or creatively?
- Are you taking a nice vacation? Possibly your first big vacation!
- Do you have your own place to call home?
- Did you finally trade in the old clunker?
- Do you see a family? That might be later down the road!
- Are you with friends?
- Are you running free and feeling accomplished?
- What do you see?

My eyes are closed and I am seeing a vision!

Ok, how did that feel? Shouldn't you do more of that? Isn't your mood lifted? **Yes! Yes! Yes!** Your vision and dream for yourself should make you smile and give you the feeling like the one when your favorite song is on, you are singing to the top of your voice and you are running through the house in your undies! Or like when you are playing the air drums pretending you are on stage with your favorite band! Just free! **Free to dream**. Some people say, "Well that dream is not practical." And I say, "Are they happy in their totally practical world?"

Your journey and dream may go through alterations, but the result of happiness and accomplishment is what we all want, no matter how it happens. If you don't have a dream or have never taken the time to fulfill one, I suggest that

today is your day! Why do you think some people don't dream? It's fear. Fear of failure or fear that the dreams won't turn out the way they dream. Most successful people will tell you that the majority of their attempts failed, but when they tried that "one more time," it worked! You must be flexible and realize the dream could play out a bit differently than you thought; however, it makes you just as happy.

Make Your Space Count

Now that we have taken time to dream and think about what we would like to see in our lives, let's talk from a job or project standpoint. If you are not looking for a job or career but want to see change in your life, then apply the following to your life.

Instead of using the words "job" or "career," use words like "projects" or "ways to make a difference." Those of you who are on the job or career path, what kind of job/career are you going to look for? Make a list of your interests, and then make a list of job/career possibilities you would like to look at and see if your interests line up with the jobs you have listed. If you are looking to add a more meaningful layer to your life, then make a list of your interests and then make a list of ways you can make a difference by using those interests.

Why should we associate true interest with the job or career that we look for? Or for the projects we are looking for? Here is a thought. If you have true interest in the job or career you choose, then wouldn't you be more likely to enjoy going to work most days? End up doing a better job? Increase the chances of getting a promotion (which increases the chances of making more money)?

Who doesn't want to make more money? Who doesn't want life to be a little easier? Does this make us greedy? No. In our case we just want to be fulfilled and increase the quality of our lives and provide for our families the best we can. If you are not looking for the job/career as we just discussed, but want to make a difference, then what you are looking for is a place you can contribute your talents or best qualities to satisfy your need to be helpful. We all are designed to help in different ways. It takes all of our unique characteristics to make this world a better place to live and work.

CHAPTER THREE

Looking Within To Create Your Plan

Discovering Talents

Let's talk about your talents. What are they? "I don't know" and "I don't have any" are not answers to this question. That just means you haven't tapped into your talents yet. First let's define a talent. As defined by Webster, it's "a natural God-given strength an individual possesses that can be lost and must be practiced." Talents are inborn reoccurring patterns of thoughts, feelings, or behaviors that can be productively applied. Talents cannot be taught. Examples would be the natural ability to play, sing, or write music; the natural ability to play sports and be athletic; the natural ability to use your hands and create art, etc. You see where I'm going with this?

Skills

Now let's define a skill. Skills are "the how-to of a role." They can be taught, and with practice, can be mastered. Can you see the benefits of putting a skill with your talent in an area you are interested in to point you into a direction of success? Being interested in what you choose to do, tapping into your talents, and combining that with a skill would be a great start when you are not sure what path to take. What if you already have a job or career and you just want to make a change? Just because we are working today doesn't mean we have found the right job and feel fulfilled. You can make a change. Happiness is worth money! Over the years I have observed many successful people, and what I noticed in this particular group was that the more they loved what they were doing the better at it they became. **They had passion!** They were making money, making a difference, and building themselves as stronger people. Money can be gone tomorrow, but who you are as a person and your contribution to society and to those around you is what will last forever.

Picture This

How do you plan to make a change? Let's keep it simple. I am going to challenge you to write down what you would like to see your life look like. Start with the big picture! For example, my big picture looks like this: I have a healthy and happy family; I want to be the best mom and wife I can be. I want to do what I am called to do. I want a wonderful home and I want to travel the world with my family. I want to make a difference in my community and do this as my job. (This is what I feel I am called to do at this time in my life.) Bringing in extra money will help to reach my goals. I want to reach specific financial goals by the time I am 40.

Now, you list smaller reachable goals that you feel would get you to your big picture. For example, my smaller goals at this time include:

- spending time reading with my girls today
- visiting their classrooms this week
- working in a date night with my husband
- talking to community leaders about the *Interview for Life* program
- setting a meeting with the school board
- talking to educators; setting up a meeting with the mayor
- meeting with my financial planner quarterly to see if I am still on target for my goal

Prioritize your list each day, week, or month as you work to accomplish your goals, and remember this is not a race. The speed at which you reach your goals is not important. **What is important is that you reach your goals and enjoy the road getting there; this is a challenge for all of us—but a challenge worth taking!**

Job vs. Career

Getting a job to bring in more money is probably on your list, so let's talk about that. **A job and a career are two different things**. A job serves a purpose, and usually you don't see yourself doing this forever. There are good things that come from your jobs.

- You build character
- You learn responsibility

- You accumulate references (very important)
- You become more self-sufficient
- You learn what it's like to work with other human beings

It's not always fun when you have to cover someone else's shift or pick up the slack when your co-workers are slacking off. It's always a challenge when you have a manager who doesn't have very good management skills or manners. Nevertheless, these opportunities teach you many qualities that will help you problem-solve for the next job. These jobs also bring in money while you are working toward the next step. A career is more of the goal. Whether you go through more schooling for this or work your way up from the bottom, the career becomes part of your life. You see yourself doing this for a long time. My hope is that your career will bring out the best in you and increase the quality of your life.

At This Point

So, what does your plan look like at this point? You should have exercised your mind by now, begun to see a vision or dream, thought about what will make you happy and full of purpose, realized that your talents and skills will be most important to tap into, and made a list of job/project possibilities that you're interested in. We know that the career is the ultimate goal; however, a job for now may be what you need to get going.

You must work on yourself before you can go out and present yourself. The next step of your plan is to take a look within.

Let's Talk About Attitude

What is an attitude? It's your state of mind when you approach a situation. It's a choice, and **you can control your attitude**. Will it be positive or negative? One leads to a healthier you, and one works against you! It's a choice. Having a positive attitude in life and on the job will always set you apart from the rest. Remember this:

> **While talent is important and knowledge is essential, the key to success is your state of mind!**

Keeping your mind sharp and healthy is your best asset. Over the years as I have researched different groups of employees. I have noticed that employees who are dependable, apply themselves with the knowledge it takes to do the job, take pride in their work, have respect for others, and smile are the ones who spread enthusiasm. Wouldn't you rather the enthusiastic person rub off on you than someone who is walking around mad at the world?

> **Attitude is so important because it shapes your mind and the ability to do your best.**

When is the last time you can say you took pride in something that you did? I ask students this all the time, and believe it or not, they usually admit they don't take pride when turning papers in to their teacher.

Respect is another important part of this picture. For many years I would ask students, "What is the number-one thing you want from your peers?" They would tell me "respect." Sit in a high school today and listen to the stories students tell about this. The hard truth is that today people are shooting each other over respect and disrespect. It is truly like a bad movie—not to mention that our students should not have to deal with this while trying to learn. It's not fair that business owners have to deal with this on the job either. Fair or not, our world is this way, so I encourage you to listen to what I'm about to say.

Question: If you give respect, then you will get respect? True or false? False! Just because you give someone respect doesn't mean that person will give it in return. You are dealing with another imperfect human who may or may not make the best choice at that moment. Think about this: instead of expecting to get respect from others, learn to focus on you. How can you give what you don't have? Do you have **self-respect**? **If you respect yourself, then your focus is on how you treat others instead of how they treat you.** When I see a person who is a real bully, I think, "Poor thing." That person has no self-respect, and therefore doesn't see how ridiculous he looks picking on the other person. He has no self-control, no obvious values, no true confidence.

> **When you have self-respect, the people around you begin to give you respect—whether you ask for it or not.**

Enthusiasm

We are still talking about working on ourselves right? Enthusiasm! Don't you love to be around happy people, or be a part of a happy occasion?

Enthusiasm is contagious.
Get excited about something!

Try it! Get fired up about something and see what people do around you. See how it makes you feel! If you are not excited in your life right now then you need to take action to make a change.

Okay, try this: **smile!** Yes, I mean you. Right now, give this book your best smile! Didn't that feel good? Now, look at someone or walk by someone and do it again! You feel good and so do they! It was free! In our classes I usually make one row of students on one side of the room show me their best smiles and then I start to point to the next row when I realize everyone's smiling from one side of the room to the other. Everyone wants to feel happy and comfortable. When you go for any kind of meeting or interview, your smile will set the tone for the next few minutes. When you smile you let someone know you are open to their presence. It's kind and welcoming. I will tell you that when I used to interview for my last company, I enjoyed so much when a person would come into my office with a smile and warm personality. I have given the recommendation to hire someone because they were professional, open to the conversation, and looked happy to be there even when their résumé lacked experience. I can teach you the job, but I can't teach you to

15

have a personality. It's up to you to use your socialization skills and manners.

Socialization Skills Emergency!

People are losing their socialization skills because everything they do is over computers or cellular phones. I am all for technology and the conveniences it gives us; however, there is still a need for you to be able to look someone in the eye, introduce yourself clearly, and shake a hand properly. Today's generations have gone to a head nod and a "what's up." This is fine for Friday night or hanging out with friends, but it is not fine for a professional meeting or an interview. **Marketing yourself** is important and can be used in *every* area of your life. It is never too late or too early to learn how to socialize properly. My daughters are ages seven and four. I teach them now the basics of speaking when they are spoken to, looking others in the eye during a conversation, and shaking their hands when they introduce themselves. There are adults I come into contact with every day who don't even do this. **You show yourself to be confident, professional, and respectful when you apply these concepts**.

CHAPTER FOUR

Keeping Perspective During the Journey

Do you think it will be easy every time you set a goal and set out to accomplish it? Only you will know that answer, but my guess is that it will take some time and hard work. How badly do you want it? How hard are you willing to work? What will it mean to you once you reach your goal? How will it change your life and make you feel once you get where you are going? We do have to be realistic about these things; however, I say **dream until your dream comes true!**

Why not? You only have this one life, and you don't know how long it will be. Make it count!

Will you get every job you interview for? I hope not. Not every job is for you, and that's why we go on interviews—to see if it's a good fit both ways. Will every project you participate in be what you are looking for? Not always. I bet you will be surprised at what you end up getting in return. I have learned that setbacks are not always bad things; most of the time they end up being a blessing. There is so much to learn from every situation if we are willing to see the lessons. I'm not saying this is easy. I've learned—and not always the easy way—but I learn.

Finding Perspective

I will tell you a brief version of how I learned about perspective. If you want to hear it in detail you will have to read a book I wrote with my daughter titled *You Can't Take My Vision!* This is a story that includes the *Interview For Life* program, but more importantly, it's about my older daughter.

In 2005 I was tired from the last several years being a full-time stockbroker and trying to juggle my growing family, so I began to pray for a new direction. I wanted to be a mom and a wife, but also had a need to feel accomplished while making a difference. I believed there could be a better way, so I could have all of those things. I didn't mind working; however, I longed to be with my daughter more and have date nights with my husband again. Our life was wonderful like many of yours—just busy, busy, busy. Sometimes it was too busy to enjoy.

During that year I had an idea. This idea eventually became the *Interview For Life* program. My mission was to improve our community and start with young people. The 2005-2006 pilot of the program took off like wildfire! The school board, the principals, the teachers, and the students loved the program, but there was just one catch. The schools were not in a position during this tough economy to pay for an extra—but needed—program. I began to raise the money through sponsors, and we were able to add the program in more schools each year. My team and I felt so blessed to have created our dream job! For the first time ever we had just as much family time as work time, and we loved our work!

Meanwhile, one Friday evening I was home opening the mail and there was a letter from our daughter's school. They were letting us know Maci had failed a routine vision screening in her left eye. Maci was 4 ½ years old and had just started pre-kindergarten at her school. My first thought was that she was fine, but might need glasses. We scheduled an appointment with a local ophthalmologist, and within two days we were headed to Texas Children's Hospital for an emergency MRI. **What I can tell you is that this wasn't in my plan**. Our life stopped in an instant. At the time, our second daughter, Ellie Kate, was only a year old. Once we settled Ellie Kate in with my parents and packed our bags, we were headed to Houston. The MRI confirmed that Maci had an optical glioma (tumor) coming through her left eye optic nerve. This is what had taken her vision away over time and caused her to fail the vision test at school. It was amazing that she never even knew. Her right eye had been overcompensating for some time. It was a miracle we found it when we did, because it was a couple of centimeters from her chiasm (where her optic nerves cross) and a few centimeters from her brain. We held her hand through chemotherapy and then a craniotomy. As her hair fell out, her dad and I began cutting our own hair shorter and shorter! During this time I was prepared to cancel the *Interview For Life* program until I could get back and continue teaching. Well, once I sent the email out to all of our teachers, they responded right away, saying, "Please do not cancel the program. We will assist your facilitators!" I have to say, that year rolled on like a well-oiled machine! *Interview For Life* didn't skip a beat or a school. That was when we realized just what an impact this was making on our schools and community. Our team would teach four days each week and I would be back in town a couple of days a week to sit in and be the helper. I want to also pat our team on the back for that year, especially Mechele Nortman, who taught with a smile every day despite her exhaustion.

The Recovery

After a seven-hour craniotomy, the tumor was removed from Maci's head and eye area. She recovered and had many months of therapy. We refused to believe this would be a negative in her life. Since the day she was diagnosed, we claim and speak positive and victorious words over her. I tell her every day that she isn't held back because she has vision only in one eye, but because of this journey and vision in one eye she is unique and powerful. She will do great things because of this and she has a big purpose! Today she is 8 and beautiful.

> One lesson I learned was that the words we speak over anyone, especially our children, will become their lifeline at some point in time.

Once Maci was on her way to recovery, she was granted a wish by the Make-A-Wish Foundation, and got to hang out with the Jonas Brothers. This experience led her to decide that what she wanted for her birthday was to ask for donations to the Make-A-Wish Foundation or St. Jude's

Children's Cancer Research instead of asking for presents. She was so proud to raise $1,300 for the children. In the summer of 2011 she put on her first Maci's Make-A-Wish and Make A Difference Festival Fundraiser and raised, after expenses, about $8,000 for the Make-A-Wish Foundation. She has a bigger vision every day and we go with it! She has dreams!

> **She is proactive in making her life meaningful!**

As a mom I wasn't always good with what happened to her. I needed to fix this for her. I would say to myself, "What would cause this? She is so healthy and sweet. What did I do wrong? What did I miss?" There were, and still are, many nights I can't sleep because I start to worry about her safety as she grows up.

Here is what I realize in the lesson of perspective. Why spend time worrying when she is healthy and beautiful and sweet and happy? She is alive! I can't put her back the way she was, and so I have to have faith that all of this is for a reason and will be used in her life for good. I have to believe and I do believe so that she will believe. **A positive perspective is hard to maintain, but we must keep our life in perspective and know that we are on a journey.** I picture a cyclist in the Tour De France when I say this: there will be hills to climb on this road that take every bit of your strength, and you question, "Can I do this?" But, around the corner there will be times you travel downhill and you don't even have to pedal, so you just enjoy the ride. A smile will be back on your face with the wind blowing through your hair.

Because of this lesson I am able to pace myself when the *Interview For Life* program is faced with a challenge or two. I continue to press on and push to get the program implemented in one place after another. **You don't quit when life gets tough; you just re-prioritize and adjust your plan.** Making a difference is healing! Keeping perspective grounds you.

CHAPTER FIVE

What Companies Are Looking For

I will keep this pretty simple: companies want committed employees. Companies want assets, not liabilities. Individuals who are fixers, not finger-pointers. **Companies want employees who not only have skill and experience to do the job, but can also fit into the company culture.** As a business owner, I want a person who has his own morals, values, and personality—because I can teach him the job, but he must have the rest. I want someone who can get the job done and increase the bottom line. That means *increase the profits!*

Make It Count

Let's be real: there are a lot of people out there who do not like the job they are in. Why? You went to the interview and obviously took the job offer. I know there are situations where the job looks great on paper and then it doesn't turn out to be what you want. There are also times when you take the job out of necessity. You have to make a choice. Do you stay or do you go? If you take the job, you should make it count! Here is the problem. Many people stay with a chip on their shoulder and their attitude stinks because they are not happy. During this time that you decide to stay and not make the best of it, you spend your time and your energy closing the door in front of you. What you need to do is make it work for you. You are already there—make it count! Make a list of what you do like about the job or company, even if there is only one thing on that list. You have to find at least one thing! Focus on what you can do in that area and talk to the manager and give ideas that explain how your talents could be used in the area you chose. This may work or may not work, but it shows you are trying and sometimes that makes a difference and changes the dynamic with your manager. We talked earlier about job vs. career. If this is a job that is part of the plan until you can get the career you are working for then your focus should be to do a good job, learn what you can, and build references while getting a paycheck. Be the best at that job because you are building character and starting good habits that will come naturally for the next job. There will be many opportunities for you to be a good example for other employees and even your managers. It's about being your best you!

Work Ethic

Let me tell you a story about a young lady who was working as a checkout clerk at a local store. My co-worker and I would go to pick up snacks and drinks for our board meetings once a month. We noticed this young lady several times because she was so friendly and professional. Once we were in a long line with several anxious customers—okay, with several *rude* and *impatient* customers! I can only imagine what this clerk's day was like most of the time. Nevertheless, she was always the same: smiling, professional, and polite. On this particular day my co-worker, who was in charge of hiring and training, said, "Let's leave our card and offer her an interview." I said, "Yes let's do it!" We waited in line, and once it was our turn to check out, we introduced ourselves to her and complimented her on her obvious work ethic. My co-worker then went on to say, "Because of how you handle customers every time we have been in here, we would like to give you our business cards and offer you an interview with our company." Now stop for a moment. Was working for a brokerage house her dream job? I don't know that answer, but what I do know is she was flattered to be in that situation. I would feel pretty proud if someone walked up to me while I was working and offered me another job.

Here is how the story played out: she did call and did get the job, which was a step up from what she was doing at her previous job. This door was opened because she kept it open. She decided to make it worth it! One job can lead you to a better one. I tell students all the time, if you are going to be there for any amount of time, then don't burn the bridge or close the door to any good opportunity that could be around the corner.

CHAPTER SIX

Professionalism

Now let's really talk about being professional. A **professional**, as defined by Webster, is someone having or showing the skill, good judgment, and polite behavior that is expected from a person who is trained to do a job well.

I will let you in on a few facts. When you get up and dress in a business or professional manner, you will be taken more seriously. Try it. If I show up in front of a class in faded jeans and a t-shirt vs. my work suit or a pair of dress pants and a nice businesslike top, which way would you take me more seriously? Do I look as smart in the faded jeans as I do in the professional clothes? Why would you judge me? I still have the same degree, work experience, and certifications no matter what I'm wearing! It's human nature to analyze someone when they walk in the room, and it's the same way when they walk into an interview. **Perception becomes reality, and it's not always fair, but it's the way it is! So, get over it and learn to play and win!**

If you want to be taken seriously, there are a few things you should know. When you are on the job, or in any public place for that matter, you should use your words carefully.

Your vocabulary says a lot about the amount of **self-respect** you have and whether you have respect for anyone else. Here are examples of situations that are most unprofessional:

- You're waiting in a business office for your appointment, and you can hear the receptionist talking about her and her boyfriend having a fight last night and plenty of the details that do not really need to be said out loud. How unprofessional!

- You're walking in a major department store with your children and the security guard who is standing in the doorway is talking to his buddy about *sex*! My seven-year-old said "Mom what was he saying about that?" The store is not where you want to have that conversation.

- You walk up to a counter and the employee is on her cellphone and holds up her hand as if to say, "just a minute." Then you are forced to listen to this conversation that makes you want to throw up!

These scenarios teach us that we should always be respectful and professional, because we do not know who is listening or observing. Your words will ultimately have an impact on the business and its customers.

OMG

Here is another situation I noticed. One morning, I was waiting in my car for my cellphone company to open for business. While I was waiting I noticed another customer, an older man, walk up to the glass door to see exactly what time the door would open. He chose to stand outside and just wait. A few minutes later I saw two employees come out of the front door and walk over to the side of the building to smoke a cigarette and drink what appeared to be an energy drink. They didn't even say "hello" or "good morning, sir, we'll be open in a minute." They just ignored him and walked on by. How unprofessional! Then two more employees came out to join in the cigarette and energy drink party. They also walked past this customer without even looking at him. I say, "why?" Why is it so hard to just be polite and professional? Technically there were no laws broken, but clearly this was unprofessional all the way around. Why go and smoke right in front of the business? That doesn't look or smell good to customers. I will not do business there again. I will drive across town to the other location because they are nice and professional. Being professional, my friends, benefits you and the business you work for. It says something about you and your company. People like to do business with good people and businesses that treat customers in a professional way. It also means *money*.

To Belt or Not to Belt

I want to share one more story. This is about a manager in an interview. I want you to remember that all day long, in every position, you are dealing with human beings. Some will be professional and some will not. How will you define who you will become? By the person you work for? They may not be professional. It's about putting your best foot forward and being your best *you* so that you will go farther. I had a student a few years ago who went on a job interview at a big technology store. We talked in class about clean dress shoes, pulling his pants up and putting on a belt, wearing a button-down dress shirt, being well groomed, giving a good handshake while speaking, and making eye contact. He was ready! Well, sometime after class and before the interview, he decided that the belt wasn't that necessary and his shoes were clean enough and shirts didn't need to be tucked in anyway. He waited and waited for his turn to be called in for the interview. Once he was called they told him he wasn't dressed appropriately and he could reschedule. At that moment he was mad! (He never realized he looked sloppy). The next day he told the class what happened and immediately started to blame the company and interviewing manager. This was going to be his excuse for not getting a job he really wanted. As a class we decided to discuss the situation. I asked him why he would let the fact that he didn't dress according to their dress code be the reason he would not get this job? Instead of blaming others, why not learn from this and go back dressed exactly the way they expected?

The benefit would be that he would get the job, enjoy the job, get paid to do the job, then do such a good job that one day he could have the manager's job. See where I am going with this?

Don't let other people stop you from being your best.

You are the only one who loses out. Well, he did go back and he did get hired and was still working there last time I went into the store.

Can you have fun on the job and still be professional? Yes. If someone wants to tell a joke or funny story, then go for it and laugh! But if you are crying, screaming, or on the floor laughing, then that's not very professional. Your words need to be appropriate. Foul language on the job is not professional, and what does it say about you anyway? There is a time and a place for everything.

I think a good way to end this section is to leave you with this thought; **professionalism shows respect.** It shows that you have self-respect and that you have respect for others. Keep that in mind.

CHAPTER SEVEN

Preparing for the Job Search

Searching for a job these days may seem like a daunting task, but there are many resources to help you. Here are a few options:

- Newspapers—Look in the local paper or on the paper's website for help-wanted advertisements.
- Company websites—If you have a specific company in mind, then a good place to start is that company's web page.
- Staffing companies—There are many staffing companies out there that can place entry-level positions to executive positions. You should schedule an appointment to discuss exactly what they can offer you and what the costs will be, if any. You always want to do your homework when dealing with any agency. A couple of good resources are the National Association of Personnel Services and the American Staffing Association. You want to choose a staffing company that specializes in the area in which you are looking to work.
- Networking—Network through your personal friends and people you do business with.

Groundwork

Talk to someone as a **mentor** who is already doing the job you would like to do. This person may not be able to give you the job; however, he or she may be able to refer you to someone who can. **Building relationships** with other people in your area of interest is a good way to make contacts and a smart way to move up in any industry.

Email your résumé to companies you are interested in, just in case they will be hiring soon. It can be very frustrating when you are looking up company after company and checking all of the career opportunities you feel qualified for and there are no openings! Do not stop there! Send in your résumé anyway. It can't hurt a thing; it might just get you a job! Most of us think to go through the human resources department, and that is a good place to start, but if you can get a department manager's name and send your résumé to his or her attention, sometimes that will start a conversation and possibly lead you to a job opening when the time is right.

You can also research through online sites that list job openings in your geographical area, such as www.monster.com, www.careerbuilder.com, www.careervoyages.gov. Helpful business publications you may be interested in, such as *Kiplinger's*, *Forbes*, and *The Wall Street Journal*, are always good resources. The most important point to keep in mind is to keep up the search. You may get tired, so take a small break and then keep sending out your résumé. Keep in mind that as the economy moves back and forth, so will the job openings.

CHAPTER EIGHT

Interview Preparation

Up to this point we have covered a lot of ground. We have been working on you as a person, polishing you on the inside. Now it's time to polish you on the outside and get you ready for the interview and professional meetings. You have figured out what you want and now your focus is to go out there and get it! The interview journey begins. The point of the interview is to set you and your best qualities apart from the rest.

Research the Company

Do the work ahead of time to see what the job description is and what the employer is looking for in an employee.

Know the position. Know the industry.

If you know this, you can show how you and your skills are just what they are looking for!

- Be able to ask a few questions regarding the company and direction of the company.

- Know what the company stands for.
- Find out what kind of community programs they are involved with.
- Learn what the future vision for the company and this position will be.
- Find out what the dress code is, and dress a step ahead of the expectation.

This shows that you have some motivation. That you want to make sure this job is a good fit for you and for the company. **By doing a little research, you are more equipped to create an intelligent conversation.**

The Résumé

The feedback from many of my students is that one of the easiest ways to create a résumé is with Microsoft Word. There are many templates to choose from. **Your résumé should be a roadmap for the interviewer**. You want your interview to be about you, so remember you have all of the answers. Many times managers are traveling and do not always remember to print and carry a copy of your résumé, so when going to an interview, have an extra copy of your résumé and cover letter. It's also good practice to have a pen or pencil, a list of professional references, driving directions to the office and the name of the person interviewing you. The name of the person interviewing you will be helpful in case you run into any unforeseen situation that would stop you from getting there on time. You should always be 10-15 minutes early; however, if something out of your control happens and causes you to run late you will want to call ahead of time. If you don't call and you don't show up, then it will be written in the file and will come back to bite you later on if you interview with that company again.

Distractions! Distractions! Distractions!

Let's talk for a minute about a few negative attributes that could be distractions during the interview. You want the interviewer to remember you for the positive and not the negative.

- Refrain from smoking before an interview. Why? Because it makes you smell bad. There is no other way to say it. If you choose to smoke, that is your decision; however, the person interviewing you may choose not to smoke; therefore, the smell of smoke will be a distraction.

- Tattoos are a common way to express your uniqueness, but to someone who doesn't care for them, they could possibly be a negative and unprofessional distraction. You don't know the company's dress policy yet, so to be safe and look professional. Cover the tattoos up for the interview. Show respect on the job and cover them up.

- Body piercings. This one is fun because some people can't even speak with tongue piercings; however, they still wear them. In the interview, if the interviewer can't understand you, what good is it for you to be there? Can you have earrings? Of course, but if you have an unusually large hole in your ear, or look like Christmas ornaments are hanging from your ear, then it could be a distraction. Minimize the distractions and show that you have self-respect, which in turn shows respect to the person taking his time to interview you.

- Too much cologne or perfume again can be a distraction.
- Grooming is a must! Can you believe I have to include this one? Yes, take a bath so you smell clean. Men, shave, please, and comb your hair. Remember to keep it out of your eyes during an interview. This goes for women and men these days. I have actually seen a few come in the office for an interview and look like they went out the night before, slept a few hours and then walked in for the interview. Not good.
- No wrinkled clothing! Today you can put your clothes on the press cycle or learn to iron; no matter how you do it, just do it!
- No chewing and smacking gum in an interview.

True story: one day I was doing an interview with a young lady and she had gum in her mouth. She was very poised and polite and the interview was going fine; however, I did notice she was talking and smacking gum and it was a little distracting, but not as distracting as when it came shooting out of her mouth and onto to my desk! "Awkward" was an understatement. We laughed and I gave her a tissue to then get her gum off my desk; nevertheless, it was a major distraction. That was time wasted on gum instead of time talking about why our company should hire her. She didn't get the job.

- Last but not least, **turn off your cellphone**. Anybody know what I'm talking about? You walk into a movie and someone has the phone to his ear. You walk into a restaurant and everyone seems to be talking on the phone instead of talking to the others at the table. Watch people driving; one out of two are on their cell phones. With all that being said, go ahead and talk on the phone, but not during an interview. Turn it off or leave it in the car.

My favorite story is one time during a class there was a student texting during my presentation. I could see her as well as hear the clicking. I could also see the student sitting next to her looking over her shoulder to see what she was doing. I think the idea that she was distracting him and now he was missing out on the information got me the most annoyed. I looked her way a couple of times as if to say, "Please stop." Still, she didn't stop, so after a few minutes I walked by her desk while I was presenting to the class. Still, she didn't stop. I then asked her to put up her phone until after class and she said she wasn't using it! Okay, I wasn't accepting that, so I sent her to the principal's office.

We are all adults here so don't act foolish or people will just dismiss you.

So have I made my points clear? No negative distractions. Do I want to change who you are or keep you from self-expressing? No and no. I want you to realize that the comfortable way you hold yourself on Friday night will not be the same as the way you conduct yourself in a professional manner. Remember that you are never wasting your time on a job interview, even if you do not get the job. Practice makes perfect! Or I should say, practice makes you more comfortable for the next interviews to come. The more interviews you go on, the more you will begin to feel at ease talking and presenting yourself. It's important to be able to speak even when you are nervous. Take any constructive criticism as an opportunity to improve yourself. Here's another point I would like you to remember. You know the saying "You only have one chance to make a first impression"? Well, in our classes I say "It's true you will make a first impression; however, if you feel like it's less than perfect, remember that you have the entire interview to make a lasting and good impression". Take the pressure off and get focused. One of the last steps we do in the *Interview For Life* program is mock interviews. It's practice. If you do a little practice before with a friend or family member, then you are more likely to sail through your interview in a confident manner and with your thoughts in order. If you really want to prepare yourself, have someone record you on a phone or with a video camera. Then you can see your body language and hear how confident you sound.

Practice Makes Perfect

Now is a good time to do a mock Interview. Things you should be aware of:

- Did you make eye contact and introduce yourself when you walked into the room.
- Did you give a good, firm handshake?
- Did you shake your leg because of nerves once you sat down? That is normal so, cross your ankles if you are a leg shaker. Remember that most people do something with their body when they get nervous. You need to know what it is that you do

so you can keep it from being a distraction during the interview.

- Your body language should show the interviewer that you are awake and listening. A smile and nod of the head once in a while show you are listening and interested in what the interviewer has to say.
- If you talk with your hands, remember to keep them in your lap or on the table. Flying hands will be a distraction.
- Another important point is not to interrupt or answer before the interviewer is finished asking you the question.
- Watch the "um, uh . . ." Take a moment to think about your answer and then speak clearly.
- Watch slang words. This never sounds professional, and in some cases the interviewer may not know what they mean.
- Always give an answer. "I don't know" is not an answer.

Think about it like this: **the interviewer has a few minutes to get to know you and see if you are right for the job.** Once you leave, the interviewer has your résumé and the lasting impression that you have given him. If you don't give answers during the interview, then how much did he get to know about you and what will he have to go on when deciding if you are right for the job? You must give him something to work with. There were many times I would practice in the mirror. I didn't have time for anything else and I would role-play right there in my bathroom mirror. Do a mock interview however you can.

CHAPTER NINE

The Interview

Get Up and Get Dressed

Okay, I hope you have had breakfast and a good night's sleep, because it's showtime! Today you are up early and you are getting dressed. Here are a few things to keep in mind.

When you dress professionally, you are more likely to be treated as a professional. How you dress sends a signal of how serious you are taking the occasion. It is true that how you dress sends a message in all situations. When you dress appropriately it shows you have self-respect and respect for the interviewer. In some situations you will need to tailor your outfit to fit the job or meeting. Asking ahead of time what the dress code is for an interview is always helpful. A rule of thumb: always dress a step above what you think the appropriate dress code is. It will never hurt your chances; it can only help.

How Will You Appear?

I will start with men first.

- If you have long bangs, then make sure your hair is out of your eyes.
- A conservative well-made suit is always nice. But what if the dress code doesn't ask for a suit? It's always a great option, but if you choose not to wear a suit, then nice dress slacks with a long-sleeve button-down shirt can be a substitution.
- Be careful of "baggy "pants.
- You want your clothes to fit you. And why a long-sleeve shirt? It looks more professional than a short sleeves.
- A tie always looks professional.
- Stay away from bright and busy patterns. This can be a distraction.
- Clean dress shoes and a belt finish you off.
- I would like to mention that the belt has an important role, which is to keep your pants up, and that is important during an interview.

Now for the women, let's go from head to toe.

- Hair out of your eyes, no heavy make-up, and your outfit should also be simple, stylish, and well-tailored.
- A skirt or pantsuit is a great option. If you choose not to wear one of these, then dress slacks or a professional-length skirt (right above your knees) with a professional-looking top will work nicely.

- Sleeveless shirts can cause distractions, so stay away from them, or use a cardigan or blazer to complete the outfit.
- Watch out for plunging necklines. You are not there to get a date; you are there to get a job! (I mean this in the nicest way possible.)
- Your shoes should be comfortable and professional. This means a closed toe is the way to go. Don't wear a higher heel than you can walk in.
- Stay away from bright crazy patterns, because you don't want to be remembered for what you wore; you want to be remembered for what you said.

Running Behind

You show up early for the interview. You look most professional. Then the receptionist says it will be a few minutes. A few minutes turns into an hour! What do you do? You may politely ask if there will still be an interview and be patient. This happens sometimes and you don't want to get fussy and lose this opportunity because you were rightfully upset. Another thing to keep in mind: be cautious of any thoughtless remarks you may make in the elevator or lobby area to another person waiting, or even to the receptionist, because it may reach the person interviewing you before you do. Manners, manners, manners.

The Grand Entrance

Take a deep breath. You can do this! Walk in confidently and give a good firm handshake. Make eye contact and speak your name clearly. Practice this over and over, and you will be surprised how smoothly your introduction will come out when you are under pressure. Practice it on other people, not just in the mirror. Why be confident? If you have confidence in yourself then the interviewer most likely will too. Why give a good, firm handshake?

Your handshake says something about you!

Are you confident? Are you professional? Are you intimidated? You want a handshake with a nice firm palm-to-palm grip. You don't want to hurt the person, and you don't want them to think you are fragile and unconfident. Practice with someone ahead of time and get their feedback.

What Are You Saying?

Why is making eye contact important? This shows confidence, honesty, and that you are present in the moment. I get asked this question a lot "Do I stare into the interviewer's eyes the entire time?" No. You don't necessarily have to lock eyes, but you want to make eye contact while you are talking, and especially when introducing yourself. You don't want to turn this into an uncomfortable stare. Why is speaking clearly and at a level that you can be understood so important? First of all, you are there to be heard, so speak up! If the interviewer can't understand your answers, then they don't have much to go on once you are gone.

Speaking up and speaking clearly shows you are sure and secure with your answers. Believe it or not, many students think this part is silly; however, when we role-play, the majority mumble their words or speak so softly that I have to say, "What's your name again?" For those of you who have unique names, remember to speak clearly, and pronounce your name so that it's understood and remembered. This can help you. If you have a unique name and the interviewer completely mispronounces it, don't be offended. Use this as an opportunity to introduce yourself again.

In the *Interview For Life* workshops all of these elements are combined to give a great impression. You must walk up to the facilitator, make eye contact, speak your name loudly and clearly, and give a good firm handshake. If you are uncomfortable with any part of this we do it again and again! Practice makes perfect!

> *Last fall we were teaching in a high school and working with the football team. All I heard was, "this will be so easy" and "this role-playing is silly." The second student in line was so nervous that he introduced himself as his buddy standing in line behind him! It was funny, but it also made a good point. Because he was actually nervous and his focus was on what he was saying to his friend, his mind took over and he introduced himself as someone else. (In his defense, both young men had the same first name but different last names.)*

When we are nervous our voices tend to get softer. We tend to speed up and mumble—which is normal. **Practice speaking slowly enough to be understood, loudly enough to be heard, and clearly enough to be remembered.**

Put Yourself Out There!

Set yourself apart from the rest! Make a lasting impression! Smile! As an interviewer I love it when someone comes into my office and it turns into a very enjoyable conversation. I say, let your personality shine. I would like to caution you on this, though. If you are a funny, jokester-type, then, yes, let your personality shine, but don't go over the line with silliness. Showing a little bit of funny will go a long way! For those of you who are more reserved and do not enjoy talking as much, then you will have to work very hard to smile and give more than yes and no answers. This needs to be a conversation between you and the interviewer. You do not want to ramble on and on with your answers, but you do want to give enough of an answer to give the interviewer a good idea of who you are and how you will be on the job.

Make Your Words Work for You

Keep this in mind: When the interviewer is describing the job duties or talks about company activities, start thinking about examples of ways you have demonstrated these kinds of duties or tasks in your past job experience. With your answer, you want to have the interviewer envisioning you in that position. Do not go on and on exaggerating your answer, but do highlight your best qualities, skills, and achievements. Some companies will put you through two or three interviews, and this is really a screening process. If you receive a phone interview, this is also used in the screening process. The rules stay the same. Be you, but be professional. Your answers should highlight you and your experience as we have just discussed. Telling stories about past experiences is a great way to leave an impression; however, don't exaggerate or make things up. Many times the interviewer will remember a story because it made an impression more so than a comment someone said. For example, if you say you are an honest and dedicated employee, make sure your story or example proves it. Your goal is to build rapport with the interviewer. Finding something in common through conversation is always a plus. Earlier we talked about why it's important to do research on the company. This way you can enter into an **intelligent conversation** that will lead to more productive conversation. Remember, never interrupt the interviewer, but show that you have done your homework. This implies you are smart and motivated. You do not want to come across as a know-it-all; that will hurt your good impression. If you do not understand the question, what do you do? Answer anyway? No. Don't be afraid to ask the interviewer to restate or clarify the question. It is much better than giving an off-the-wall answer that could make you look less than awake.

Game On

You enter the interview, introduce yourself, and wait to sit when the interviewer sits. Did you catch that one? It is always a good idea to wait until the interviewer sits down before you sit down. This is just one extra display of manners that shows respect. Always refer to the interviewer by their last name unless they say otherwise. Again, showing respect shows you have self-respect as well.

- Show some enthusiasm!
- Act happy to be there
- Enjoy the opportunity before you

If you are asked difficult questions, use them to showcase your problem-solving skills. If you are asked a question that has stumped you, you can't think! Take a minute to breathe, think through the question and give the best confident answer you can. Many interviewers admit that they ask especially tough questions to see if the candidate can handle pressure and what he/she would do under pressure. Many times there is not a right or wrong answer, so give them something about you to go on.

Have a few questions prepared for the interviewer. By doing a little research ahead of time, come up with a few questions, possibly about the future of the company, or its product line, or how long they are going to continue to interview for this position. Ask the manager what made him choose this company and what he likes the best about his job. These are examples that will help you come up with your own ideas. Asking a few questions lets the interviewer know you are interested in the opportunity and want to be considered for the job.

The Grand Exit

What should the interview exit look like? I'm sure you guessed it. A lot like the entrance. Stand up, extend your hand with a good, firm handshake, and thank the interviewer for their time. I would always follow up with, "So when can I expect to hear from you? I feel like this is a great fit for me and for the company" (if you do in fact feel that way).

The Follow-Up Plan

A few days after the interview send a thank-you card addressed to the person who interviewed you. This is why you should ask for his or her business card once the interview is coming to an end. If the interviewer does not have a card, then write their name down on your piece of paper and spell it correctly. The thank-you card shows that you are professional and also puts your name across their desk one more time. This could also make a difference in who gets the job. One more benefit of sending a thank-you card or brief thank-you letter is that later down the road, the company may look in the file once a job opening comes available—and remember you. You don't want to appear pushy or too anxious, so before making another attempt I would wait a couple of weeks. I also get asked, "Is it appropriate to send a thank-you email?" Yes. We are in the age of technology, and a brief thank-you and "When can I expect to hear from you?" works just fine. Most HR representatives would rather respond over email than have to make a phone call. They are busy enough. Remember you are probably not the only one interviewing for the position. Make it count!

Plan B

It is a good idea to interview with several companies while searching for your job. This process can take some time, so putting more eggs in your basket will increase the chances of your getting a job sooner rather than later.

The Job Offer

If it was a good fit for both of you, then accept the position and bring your game! If you decide it is not the job for you, then thank them for the opportunity and politely decline the offer. If you are left a message, please call them back. Never refuse to return the call. It will be written in your temporary file and you never know when you might end up there again looking for a job. If you have been interviewing with more than one company, and multiple job offers come in, then what do you do? You interview with Company A and Company B. You decide A is your choice, so thank B and tell them the truth—that you have accepted an offer from another company and feel the other position is a better fit for you at this time, but you really appreciate the offer. In classes I love to ask this question: If you are in this situation, what do you do? Can you believe some students say they just don't call Company B back! You are always too young to burn a bridge. You never know when life might lead you back to that point.

Technology No-No's

In everything we do technology seems to help us! I want you to keep something in mind; **the same technology that can help you search and prepare for the job can also be used to get you fired from the job.** Today with Facebook, Twitter, cameras and video on every cellphone, keep in mind that if you do anything that could be perceived as inappropriate, unprofessional behavior, it can easily be put out there for everyone to see—including your employer or potential employer. Some HR departments even hire employees to check for this kind of thing. A company's reputation can be hurt by irresponsible employees. Once you press *send* or *post*, it's out there forever. This is a good time to think about what you stand for and what you as a person have to contribute to a company or team.

The Phone Interview

If you are going to have a phone interview remember a few things:

- You must come across enthusiastic and motivated as you are discussing the career opportunity. Allow your enthusiasm to show through your choice of words and the way you say them.
- Follow the same guidelines we discussed earlier on preparing for the face-to-face interview to ensure an intelligent conversation.
- Try to avoid this interview over a cellphone. A landline is clearer and less likely to cut out, causing the interviewer to miss something important you say.
- Be there when they call!

This can be a way of weeding out or screening applicants. This can also be the most efficient way for the company to talk to you first if you are located states apart. It is common for some companies to put you through a couple of phone interviews before a face-to-face interview.

The same principles apply if the interview is over Skype or any other form of web conferencing. Remember to dress for the interview and apply all of the previous points that we have discussed.

CHAPTER TEN

All About the Questions

Here are a few tips to remember when you are answering interview questions:

- In your answers make sure you give examples of your skills and experience.
  Think about how they will help you with this particular job position.
- Don't sound arrogant; give confident answers.
- Talk about what you have learned from your previous experiences and how you can use this on the new job.
- Know your strengths and know your weaknesses.
- Keep a positive and optimistic spin on your choice of words.
- Know what sets you apart from the rest regarding your work ethic.
- Be sure to stick with work-related explanations instead of personal ones, if at all possible.
- If you are asked a question that could have a potential negative answer then focus on positive points that can be learned or drawn from the example.
- Give examples of problem-solving situations.

- You don't need to discuss your entire work history; the interviewer is looking for a reason you think you would be a good fit for the position based on your recent work experiences.
- The interviewer only has a few minutes to get to know you and see if you are the right fit for the job and company environment, so give them something to think about.
- Have strong professional references. If you are just starting out, then list teachers, professors, or any managers you have a good relationship with.
- Do not ask about salary or pay right away. Once there is an agreement that you can add value to the company, then you may bring this up for discussion. However, the pay rate should be included in your offer.
- Use the toughest questions as an opportunity to show you can remain calm and work through a stressful situation.

As we discussed earlier, my intent is not to give you lots of questions and answers, but to encourage you, motivate you, and challenge you to think. Think about what you want in life, in a job, and plan to get it! I want you to think through situations because *you have the answers*. The interview is about you.

Sample Questions:

I suggest you take time to write these questions down along with your answers. This will get you thinking before the interview and you will have fresh examples on your mind for when the interview comes.

Why should I hire you? Be ready to give one or two good examples that include your skills and experience. This could come from your previous job. Show how this would make you an asset to the new job. Remember to do your homework and know what they are looking for in an employee by knowing the job description ahead of time.

Give me a time when you were either on the job or in school and you were faced with a challenge. I want to know what the challenge was, what steps you took to resolve it and how it ended up. Here you need to think of a time where your contribution made a difference. Tell what steps you took to resolve the conflict or improve the situation. Finish it off by telling how the situation ended up. You should keep in mind that this question is asking for your problem-solving skills in three steps.

What are your strengths? You should have an idea by now of what you do best. Think of your top three strengths and how they can be applied to the job position you are interviewing for. Give an example of how your strengths will be used on this job you are interviewing for.

What are your weaknesses? We all have them, so pick one area you know you can improve in. You can also tell about a time that this weakness caused you to do less than your best on a job and what you have done since then to strengthen the weakness.

Do you like a team setting or to work on your own? Be honest and give your preference; however, give an example of a time when you worked well in both situations. You are giving them your honest answer but you are also showing that you can be flexible and work in either environment when necessary.

How many times did you miss work on your last job? Be honest, because they may already know. This is an opportunity to highlight how much of a dedicated employee you are (if the number of days missed is low). If you missed several days you will want to give a brief explanation of why you missed work, but focus on what you did to make up any time missed.

Why did you choose to interview with our company? This is a great time to show what research you have done on the company. Complimenting the manager on company accomplishments or areas of focus that are also important to you will start a good conversation.

Tell me about a time you accomplished something really big. Again, this is a great time to highlight your biggest accomplishment. The example must give him an idea of how that accomplishment would make a difference on his job. Be factual, not braggy.

Give me an example of a time when you didn't get along with a co-worker? If there is a time, briefly mention it; however, focus on what you did to solve the problem, making the work environment productive for both you and your co-workers.

How important do you think customer service is? Here you want to show that you are able to set aside personal feelings and react professionally. You want to show you can resolve conflict and keep the customer happy so she will continue to do business with you and the company you represent. Give an example of a time you were in this situation.

How important is leadership to you? Think of a time when as a result of great leadership you were able to perform above and beyond your expectation. Be able to express how you can learn from leadership and how you would perform if you were given a leadership role.

How important do you think a positive work environment is? Give an example of a time where you contributed to making your work environment positive and productive. How can a company benefit from happy employees in a positive, productive workplace?

How are your communication skills? If communication is your strength, then give an example of how you used this skill to improve a work situation. If this is not your strong point, explain the steps you are taking to improve in this area and be sure to state that you see the benefit in good communication skills on the job.

What were your grades like in school? If your grades were good or great, then let them know, but focus on the study skills you had to develop to keep your grades on track. Let them hear about the focus and dedication it took to meet your goals. If your grades were not the best, then this is a great opportunity to show how you had to remain focused and positive with an attitude of "I will not fail!" There is a lot to be said for someone who has a dream and does not quit. Tell your story briefly.

Why do you want to leave your current job or position?
Think of the benefits of moving on to the next job or position. Focus your answers on what you have learned from the current job or position and how this position you are interviewing for is one step closer to your overall goal. Do not focus your answer on all of the imperfect things about your current job, manager, or workplace. Keep your answer focused on the positive effects that this change will create. State that you appreciate where you are; however, you are excited about future opportunities.

CHAPTER ELEVEN

Planning for Your Financial Future

You are never too young to start thinking about your financial future. If you are old enough to work, you are old enough to start good spending habits and start saving a little at a time. Many times I have been asked, "Why do I need to think about this now? I have plenty of time to save." What you don't realize when you are younger is that you are at the perfect age to start saving. You have less to pay for at that time than you ever will. Time is your friend, and you are entering the best earning years of your life. Get excited! As you get older and start making more money, then you begin buying bigger toys and fancier cars. If you start good habits now, it will be easier to save and spend wisely as you go on.

Go back to your dream. What did it look like? How do you think you paid for the things in your dream? Obviously time with your family and friends doesn't cost anything, but the house you all gather in or the car that drives you to dinner, the clothes you wore to dinner and the cell phone you used to call your friends—all these cost something. **We take a lot for granted, so it's important to stop and really**

think about what kind of life you want and what it may cost. Be prepared so you will not end up in a bind or broke. A great goal is to live free of debt and financially sound.

Debt

What is debt? Wikipedia says, "A debt is created when a creditor agrees to lend a sum of assets to a debtor." Debt is usually granted with **expected repayment**. In modern society, in most cases, this includes **repayment of the original sum, plus interest**. Start a wish list and include what the costs will be. Make a plan to reach your goal.

Many times young people are approved for credit cards. A credit card benefits the card company first and only benefits you if you pay it off in full at the end of the month—assuming you do have the money to pay it off. Do not be fooled and think it is free money. Someone will pay the bill. If you do not pay your bill and end up in bad debt, then your credit score will be affected. This is serious business!

You will feel it the most down the road when you want to buy something as important as a house or a car, and you get denied because your credit score is not good enough. Build good credit. Don't try to buy things if you can't afford them, and pay your bills on time when they come in.

I get asked, "Why do I need a savings account?" Because if you put a little at a time in your savings account, it will earn a little interest (and any interest is better than none). Then, one day you will look back and see that you have accumulated quite a bit of money. Another benefit is, if you have an emergency, you will have money set aside to get you through. Keeping your savings "out of sight and out of mind" helps you save until you *need* the money for something important.

I encourage you to sign up for your company's 401(k) retirement plan. What is that? It's a company-sponsored retirement account. This is where you will contribute a certain amount and your company will also contribute a certain amount. It's free money, so take it! This money is only to be used once you retire. That may sound far off in the future, but the truth is, it takes that long to build your retirement—so start now. If you are not with a company that offers this type of plan, you can open an IRA (Individual Retirement Account). This account is offered through brokerage houses and most banks. There is a range of investments from conservative to aggressive, so you will want to get with a representative and plan according to your risk profile.

I have had many people shy away from this conversation because they were not educated properly. Take the time to talk to someone who is properly educated in this area or a financial planner, and learn so you will know what is going on with your money. Make good decisions now that will make your life easier as you travel along your journey.

CHAPTER TWELVE

Using Your Success To Make a Difference!

At this point you have asked yourself tough questions to figure out what your dreams are and what you want out of your life. You have a dream! You know you are talented and capable of learning a skill or many skills. You are creating a plan! You are reminded to keep perspective during this journey, and you are off to start your career or get a job to reach your goal. You are prepared for the interview and know the importance of professionalism. **You have what it takes to be amazing, personally and professionally.** You are on your way!

Seeds of Greatness!

Now it's your turn to give this to someone else. Use what you have learned to make a difference in others in your community and the little world around you.

> **Sometimes it just takes planting that one seed to grow greatness in another person.**

Ask yourself, how am I using what it is that I do to make a difference? This week, have you done something or helped with a project that will impact another person? This month? This year? Each and every one of you has a gift and can change the world or someone's world in a special way. It's a choice. When we feel like we have something worth giving is when we as people begin to reach out. Now is your time. You will be amazed at how much your life is enriched by giving to others. When the plan is to help others or make a difference, you will be surprised that many times we are the ones who gain so much.

One last question before you go: what is "fun" to you? What is "happy" to you? Stop and think about these answers. Do the answers satisfy your desire to be needed on the job and in your life? **Are you making your space on this earth count?** Enjoy your life and get fun from your job. Cherish your loved ones and appreciate the time you have. No job or life will be perfect, but if you keep a good attitude and use these experiences to build your bright future, then you will enjoy this journey more and help someone else and make a difference along the way. Isn't that why we are here? Sometimes we all get so focused on our own plan that we forget to step back and realize His plan. I challenge you to live your best life!

For information about the *Interview For Life* Programs, visit interviewforlife.com. For requests to have the program brought to your high school or college, send your request through the contact tab on the *Interview For Life* website.

NOTES

NOTES

NOTES

NOTES

NOTES